GW01316229

Simple Valentine Crochet Patterns

Crochet Projects for Valentine's Day

Copyright © 2021

All rights reserved.

DEDICATION

Contents

Puppy Amigurumi – Tammy 1

Box of Chocolates 17

Heart Motif Infinity Scarf Crochet 29

Lovebirds 35

Heart Gift Bag 43

Puppy Amigurumi – Tammy

I "Ruff" U, Tammy the amigurumi puppy is here to wish you all Happy Valentine's Day!!! Designed by the utterly talented Amigurumi-an, Lee Mei Li of AmiguruMEI, Tammy the cuteness overload amigurumi puppy is going to melt everybody's heart. Crochet it and give it to your loved one today. Let Tammy be the cupid of the most romantic day of the year!

This little cutie puppy amigurumi measures about 3" tall, crochet with cyan and white yarns. You will need to know how to change the yarn colors while single crochet in a round.

Materials

Acrylic Yarn in white, cyan, and fuchsia

Crochet thread in black

2 x 4mm black brads

White felt

Pink blush

Tools

3mm hook

Darning needle

Polyester fiberfill

Instructions

Abbreviations

Ch: chain

Sc: single crochet

Dc: double crochet

Head

Start with cyan yarn.

Round 1: Sc 6 in magic ring {6}.

Round 2: [Inc] around {12}.

Round 3: [Inc, sc 1] around {18}.

Round 4: [Inc, sc 2] around {24}.

Round 5: [Inc, sc 3] around {30}.

Round 6: [Inc, sc 4] around {36}.

Round 7-8: Sc around {36}.

Round 9: Sc in the next 12 sts, change to white yarn and sc in the next 5 sts, change back to cyan and sc in the next 2sts, change to white and sc in the next 5 sts then change to cyan and sc in the next 12 sts {36}.

Round 10-11: Sc in the next 12 sts (cyan), sc in the next 12 sts (white), sc in the next 12 sts (cyan) {36}.

Round 12: Change to white yarn. Sc around {36}.

Round 13: [Inv dec, sc 4] around {30}.

Round 14: [Inv dec, sc 3] around {24}.

Round 15: [Inv dec, sc 2] around {18}.

Stuff.

Round 16: [Inv dec, sc 1] around {12}.

Round 17: [Inv dec] around {6}.

Fasten off and weave in ends. Leave a long end.

To make eye indentations: Using the remaining end of the yarn, thread it through a stitch at the left side of the head below Round 11. Make a horizontal backstitch. Repeat on the other side. Bring yarn to the bottom of the head and trim excess.

Body

Start with white yarn.

Round 1: Sc 6 in magic ring {6}.

Round 2: [Inc] around {12}.

Round 3: [Inc, sc 1] around {18}.

Round 4: [Inc, sc 2] around {24}.

Round 5: Sc in the next 20 sts, change to cyan yarn and sc in the next 4 sts {24}.

Round 6-9: Sc in the next 4 sts (cyan), sc in the next 16 sts (white), sc in the next 4 sts (cyan) {24}.

Round 10: In the first 4 sts, inv dec, sc 2 (cyan). In the next 16 sts, inv dec, sc 2 (white). In the last 4 sts, inv dec, sc 2 (cyan) {18}.

Fasten off and leave a long end for sewing.

Ears

Make 2 with cyan yarn.

Round 1: Sc 6 in magic ring {6}.

Round 2: [Inc] around {12}.

Round 3-10: Sc around {12}.

Fasten off and leave a long tail for sewing.

Muzzle

Use white yarn.

Round 1: Sc 5 in magic ring {5}.

Round 2: Sc around {10}.

Fasten off and leave a long tail for sewing.

Arms

Make 2 with white yarn.

Round 1: Sc 6 in magic ring {6}.

Round 2-5: Sc around {6}.

Fasten off and leave a long tail for sewing.

Feet

Make 2 with white yarn.

Round 1: Sc 6 in magic ring {6}.

Round 2: [Inc] around {12}.

Round 3: Sc around {12}.

Round 4: [Inv dec] around {6}.

Fasten off and weave in ends but leave a long tail for sewing.

Flatten.

Tail

Use white yarn.

Round 1: Sc 3 in magic ring {3}.

Round 2: [Inc] around {6}.

Round 3: [Inc, sc 1] around {9}.

Round 4: Sc around {9}.

Round 5: [Inv dec, sc 1] around {6}.

Round 6: Sc around {6}.

Fasten off and leave a long tail for sewing.

Heart

Use fuchsia yarn. This pattern is made by joining two pieces together.

To make the first piece:

Round 1: Sc 8 in magic ring {8}.

Round 2-3: Sc around {8}.

Fasten off and leave a long end for sewing.

To make the second piece:

Round 1: Sc 8 in magic ring {8}.

Round 2-3: Sc around {8}.

Round 4: This will be where the two pieces join. Sc in the next 6 sts, then continue on to sc in the sts of the first heart piece. When you reach back to the second heart piece, sc in the remaining sts {16}. (you may use excess yarn from the first piece to tighten any gaps between the two pieces)

Round 5: [Inv dec, sc 2] around {12}.

Round 6: [Inv dec, sc 1] around {8}.

Round 7: [Inv dec] around {4}.

Fasten off and weave in ends.

Leave a long end for sewing.

Assembly

1. Sew the muzzle onto the head.

2. Using black crochet thread, sew on the nose using a series of horizontal backstitches. We made a total of 11 backstitches for tiny Tammy.

3. With the remaining black crochet thread, sew a W shape for the lips. Make tiny backstitch loops near the curves to turn it into a smile. Try using your darning needle to push the curves into place.

4. Cut white felt into two small crescent shapes, matching the size of the black brads. Pair them up with the black brads and glue them onto where the eye indentations are.

5. Sew on the body, arms, feet, ears, and tail.

6. Sew heart onto the front of the body.

7. Add a pop of blush onto Tammy's cheeks.

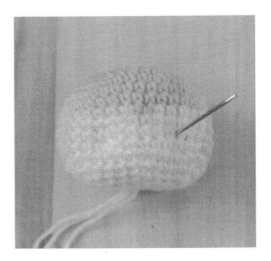

Make eye indentations by sewing a horizontal backstitch at a spot on the right and left side of the head below Round 11.

Sew the muzzle onto the head.

Glue on black brads as eyes.

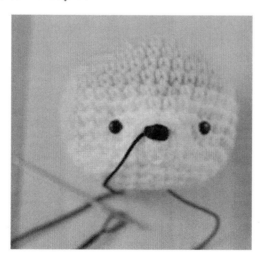

Sew on the nose using a series of horizontal backstitches.

Sew on the lips.

Make tiny backstitch loops near the curves to turn it into a smile.

Try using your darning needle to push the curves into place.

Pins parts to the body and sew them on.

Sew heart onto the front of the body of puppy amigurumi.

Make eye indentations by sewing a horizontal backstitch at a spot on the right and left side of the head below Round 11.

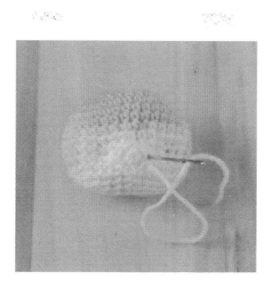

Sew the muzzle onto the head.

Glue on black brads as eyes.

Sew on the nose using a series of horizontal backstitches.

Sew on the lips.

Make tiny backstitch loops near the curves to turn it into a smile.

Try using your darning needle to push the curves into place.

Pins parts to the body and sew them on.

Sew heart onto the front of the body of puppy amigurumi.

Box of Chocolates

This Valentine's Day, whip up some easy and adorable chocolates for your loved ones. Check out these step-by-step instructions on how to crochet your own chocolates and box.

Directions: Easy

Size: 16 x 12.5 cm (6 x 5 inches)

Abbreviations:

ch: chain

sl st: slip stitch

sc: single crochet

scinc: single crochet increase

scdec: single crochet decrease

sc4tog: single crochet four together

dc: double crochet

tr: treble (triple) crochet

st(s): stitch(es)

Special Stitch:

Insert hook in next stitch, yarn over, pull loop through stitch four times. Yarn over and draw yarn through all five loops on hook. Completed sc4tog — three stitches decreased.

Materials:

Worsted-weight yarn in red (ca. 30 grams) for box, various yarn colors for chocolates (I used brown, off-white, pastel pink and cyclamen)

Gold-fingering yarn for box edging and small heart

Size 4.5 mm (7) and 3 mm (D) crochet hooks

Cardboard

Red felt

Glue

Toy stuffing

Accessories to embroider chocolates (yarn, beads, etc.)

12 petit-four cups

Stitch marker (optional)

The pattern box

Bottom of box, with red yarn and 4.5 mm (7) hook.

Note: Work in continuous rounds for sides; do not join or turn unless otherwise indicated. Sc evenly around all four sides of base.

Ch 16, sc in second ch from hook up to the end (15).

Report ad

Repeat until your piece measures 14 cm (5.5 inches) from beginning.

Do not fasten off.

R1: Working through back loops, sc in each st around.

R2 – 5: Sc in each st around. Fasten off.

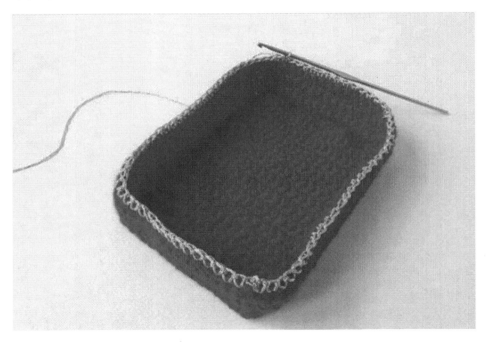

Attach gold-fingering yarn in any corner space with 3 mm (D) hook.

R1: Sc around in each space, scdec in each corner space.

Fasten off.

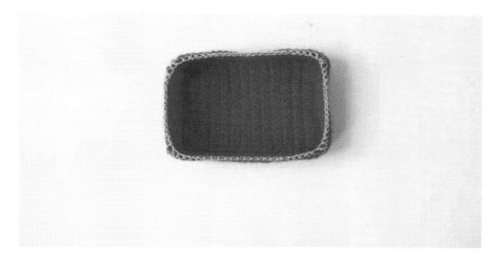

Lid (make as bottom)

With red yarn and 4.5 mm (7) hook.

Ch 20, sc in second ch from hook up to the end (19).

Repeat until your piece measures 16 cm (6 inches) from beginning.

Do not fasten off.

Note: Work in continuous rnds for sides; do not join or turn unless otherwise indicated.

Sc evenly around all four sides of base.

R1 Working through back loops, sc in each st around, sc4tog in each corner space.

R2 – 5: Sc in each st around. Fasten off.

Attach gold-fingering yarn in any corner space (in front loops of the first round you started making the sides) and with 3 mm (D) hook.

R1: Sc around in each space, scdec in each corner space.

Fasten off.

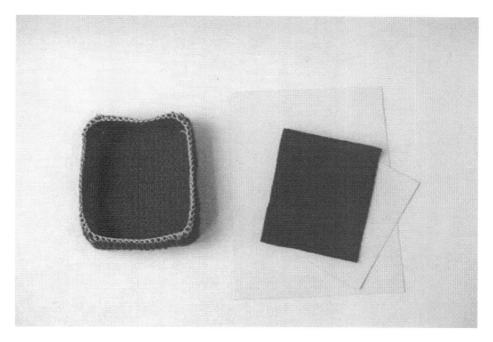

Cut two pieces of cardboard according to the measurements of your box.

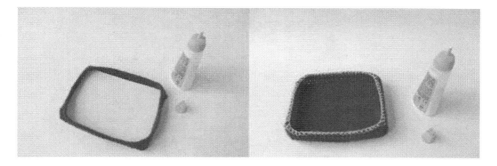

Glue each cardboard piece to the inner bottom and lid of the box.

Once dry, cut some red felt, measuring exactly the same as your cardboard, and glue it on the cardboard pieces. Set aside to dry.

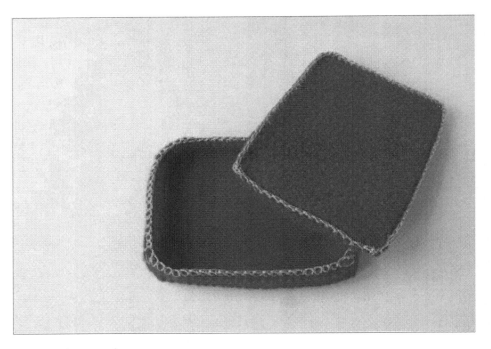

Heart decoration

With gold fingering-yarn and hook of your choice.*

You can use any hook size you want to make the hearts. If you want a larger one, use a 4 mm (G), and if you want a smaller one, use a 2 mm (B/1) hook. I went for the middle size and used a 3 mm (D) hook.

Ch 4 and make 3 tr in the fourth ch from hook. *All stitches will be worked in the fourth ch from hook.*

Three dc, ch 1, 1 tr, ch 1, 3 dc, 3 tr, ch 3 and join with sl st to center of heart.

Sew heart on lid. You can make one or more hearts.

Chocolates

With yarn color of your choice and 3 mm (D) hook.

Ch 2 or make a magic loop.

R1: 6 sc in second ch from hook (6).

R2: 2 sc in each st around (12).

R3: *1 sc , scinc,* repeat from *5 times (18).

R4: sc around (18).

R5: *1 sc , scdec,* repeat from *5 times (12).

R6: *dec*, repeat from *5 times (6).

Fasten off.

Make 12-inch various colors or use just one color.

Decorate your chocolates by embroidering different shapes using yarn, or add some beads.

To make the swirl, ch 18 and sew on top of chocolate.

Complete

Place your chocolates in some petit-four cups and inside your box.

Heart Motif Infinity Scarf Crochet

With Valentine's Day around the corner, it's the perfect time to share this heart motif infinity scarf crochet pattern. This is a great adult craft project, allowing you to challenge your inner crochet skills. This scarf pattern is the perfect length to keep you cozy during the frigid months of January and February, plus the little hearts are just so pretty!

What you need to make this infinity scarf crochet pattern:

H hook

2 100g skeins of Medium Weight gray yarn

4 colors of scrap yarn (several yards long)

Scissors

Abbreviations: American Terms

Ch   —Chain

Sc		— Single		Crochet
Dc		— Double		Crochet
Sl	st		— Slip	Stitch
Bpdc	— Back	Post	Double	Crochet
Fpdc	— Front	post	Double	Crochet
Sk — Skip				

Approx. finished measurements: 6" x 50"

Special   Stitch:
3-dc cluster: Yarn over, insert hook. Yarn over, pull through st (3 loops on hook). Yarn over, pull through first 2 loops (2 loops remaining on hook). Yarn over, insert in same st. Yarn over, pull through. Yarn over, pull through first 2 loops (3 loops remaining on hook). Yarn over, insert into same st. Yarn over, pull through. Yarn over and pull through first 2 loops. Yarn over, pull through all 4 remaining loops. *If it's easier to understand, it's basically a dc3tog worked all in the same st.*

Ch 198. Sl st into 1st ch, careful not to twist. Should be just under 50" long.

1. Ch 2. Dc in each st around. Join with a sl st (198 sts)

2. – 3. Ch 2. Fpdc around 1st dc from previous round. Bpdc around next one. Alternate fpdc and bpdc all around. Join with sl st. (198 sts) (On row 3, be sure you are working a fpdc around a previous fpdc, and not around a bpdc, to make it looked ribbed.) Join 2nd color.

4. Ch 1. 4 dc in same st. *Ch 1. Sk 5 sts. 4 dc in next st.* work 32 times. Ch 1. Join with 1st dc. (165 sts).

30

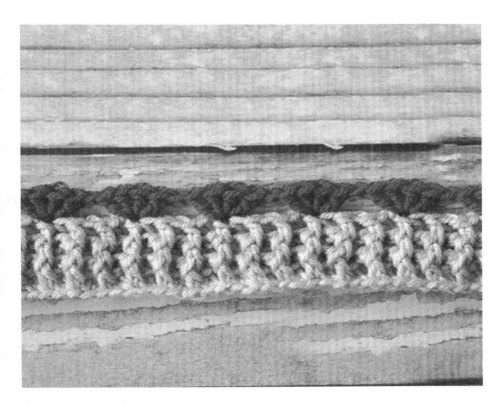

Bring up 1st color.

5. Ch 2. Sc in middle of shell (not in a st, in the space between the stitches). Ch 2. Work a 3-dc cluster in the 3rd st of the 5 skipped sts from the previous round. *Ch 2. Sc in middle sp of shell. Ch 2. Work a 3-dc cluster in 3rd sk st from previous round* repeat all around the hat. Join with a sl st with first chain. (198 sts)

6. Ch 2. Dc in each st around. Join with a sl st. (198 sts).

Tip: If you found you dropped a stitch in row 5, it is easiest to add them into this row instead of pulling out your work.

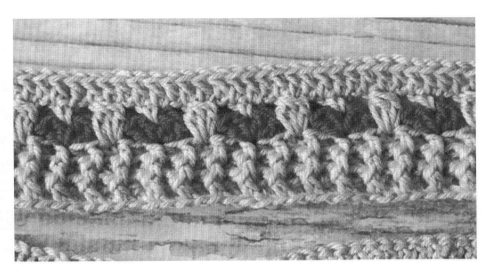

7. – 15. Repeat rows 4 – 6 respectively, joining a different color each time you work the hearts row.

16. – 17. Ch 2. Fpdc around 1st dc from previous round. Bpdc around next one. Alternate fpdc and bpdc all around. Join with sl st. (198 sts) (On row 17, be sure you are working a fpdc around a previous fpdc, and not around a bpdc, to make it looked ribbed.)

Now you have an adorable heart accented puppy love infinity scarf! This would make a lovely Valentine's Day craft or gift for someone you love.

Lovebirds

Look at these two! Such an adorable couple. Hope you enjoy crocheting these two cuties! This project works up quick and perfect for amigurumi beginners as it's super easy to make.

You will need:

4mm crochet hook

8 ply (DK/ Light Worsted) acrylic yarn (in teal and orange)

small amount of yellow and pink yarn

2 x 12mm plastic safety eyes

toy stuffing

yarn needle

scissors

Abbreviations (US Terminology)

rnd – round

sc – single crochet

inc – increase (2 sc in one stitch)

dec – single crochet 2 together

rep – repeat

PATTERN NOTES

You will be crocheting in spirals.

Use the invisible decrease technique – if you're not familiar with this decrease, a regular single crochet decrease is perfectly fine to do.

When finished, the bird is roughly 10cm (4 inches) tall.

BODY (with teal or orange yarn)

Rnd	1:	6	sc	in	magic	ring	(6)
Rnd	2:	2	sc	in	each	st	around	(12)
Rnd	3:	Sc	1,	inc;	rep	6	times	(18)
Rnd	4:	Sc	2,	inc;	rep	6	times	(24)
Rnd	5:	Sc	3,	inc;	rep	6	times	(30)
Rnd	6:	Sc	4,	inc;	rep	6	times	(36)
Rnds	7	–	10:	Sc	around	(36)
Rnd	11:	Sc	4,	dec;	rep	6	times	(30)
Rnd	12:	Sc	around	(30)
Rnd	13:	Sc	4,	inc;	rep	6	times	(36)
Rnd	14:	Sc	5,	inc;	rep	6	times	(42)
Rnds	15	–	19:	Sc	around	(42)

Attach eyes between Rounds 11 & 12, 3 stitches apart.

Rnd	20:	Sc	5,	dec;	rep	6	times	(36)
Rnd	21:	Sc	4,	dec;	rep	6	times	(30)
Rnd	22:	Sc	3,	dec;	rep	6	times	(24)

Begin to stuff firmly.

Rnd	23:	Sc	2,	dec;	rep	6	times	(18)
Rnd	24:	Sc	1,	dec;	rep	6	times	(12)

Continue to stuff firmly.

Rnd 25: Dec 6 times (6)

Fasten off and leave a long tail end. To close the body, weave tail end through all 6 stitches in the front loops only then pull. Weave in and hide tail end in the body. Scroll down to see pictures for reference.

WINGS (with teal or orange yarn) (MAKE 2)

Rnd	1:	6	sc	in	magic	ring	(6)

Rnd 2: 2 sc in each st around (12)

Rnds 3 – 4: Sc around (12)

Rnd 5: Sc 4, dec; rep 2 times (10)

Fasten off and leave long tail end for sewing.

TAIL (with teal or orange yarn)

Rnd 1: 5 sc in magic ring (5)

Rnd 2: Sc around (5)

Rnd 3: 2 sc in each st around (10)

Rnd 4: Sc around (10)

Fasten off and leave long tail end for sewing.

ASSEMBLY

Flatten wings and sew onto the sides of the body (between Rounds 13 & 14). Weave in and hide yarn end.

Flatten tail and sew onto the lower rear of the body (between Rounds 18 & 19). Weave in and hide yarn end.

Using yellow yarn, embroider the beak. Weave in and hide yarn end.

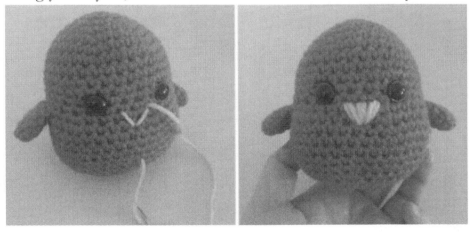

Using pink yarn, embroider the blush. Don't forget to weave in and hide   yarn   end!

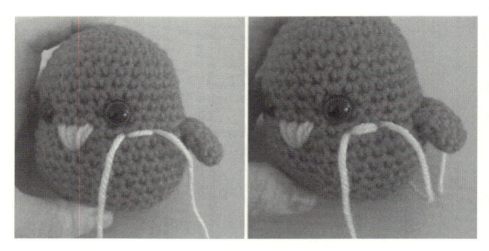

Loop through a couple of strands of yellow yarn on top of the head.

Insert hook in the centre then out through one stitch hole. With the hook, grab a few   strands   of   yellow   yarn.

Yarn over and pull through the loop. Cut off yarn to preferred length.

HOW TO CLOSE

I learned of this wonderful closing/finishing technique from June at PlanetJune.

After the last round, Fasten off as per normal. Coming in from the centre always, weave in yarn tail end through the front loops of each stitch then pull the tail end carefully.

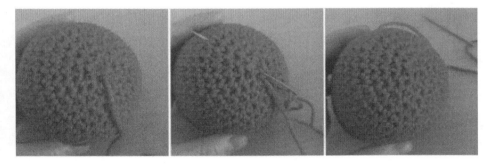

It should now close. Insert the needle in the centre again then weave in and hide the yarn tail through the piece several times. Cut off the excess yarn.

See how they're so chubby looking and a little unusual! Make sure to make two lovebirds so they're never alone!!

Heart Gift Bag

Materials;

30g of DK yarn for the main colour of the bag. Small amount of contrasting piece of yarn for the heart. Here, Yeoman Yarn's Panama DK in Haze and Fiesta have been used
3.5mm hook
Approx 50cm of ribbon.

Stitches used;

ch = chain

dc = double crochet (sc in US terms)

tr = treble crochet (dc in US terms)

Abbreviations;

frm = from

til = until

rpt = repeat

Dimensions;

Finished bag size approx 14cm x 10cm (5.5" x 3.5")

Inside pouch size approx 10cm x 9cm (4" x 3.25")

With your main colour yarn, work 17ch plus 1ch for turning.

Row 1;

In 2nd ch frm hook work 1dc, 1dc in each ch til end. Turn.

Row 2;

1ch, 1dc in 1st dc, 1dc in each dc across til end. Turn.

Row 3-5;

Rpt row 2. Turn.

Row 6;

3ch (represents 1tr, 1ch), miss 1st dc, * 1tr in next dc, 1ch, miss 1 dc,* rpt frm * til end working last tr in turning ch (9 1ch spaces). Turn.

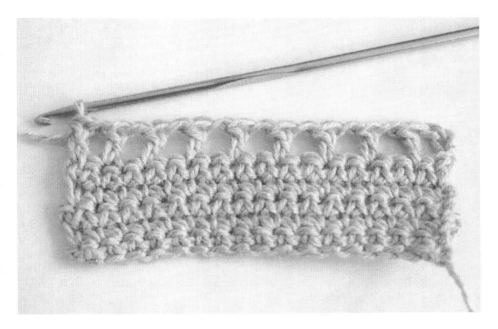

Row 7;

1ch, 1dc in 1st 1 ch space, 1dc in each tr and 1 ch space til end working last dc in top of turning ch. Turn (17dc in total).

Row 8-31;

1ch, 1dc in each dc across til end. Turn.

Row 32-41;

Work from graph below, snaking your way up, making sure to work 1ch at the beginning of each row for turning.

1 square = 1 dc

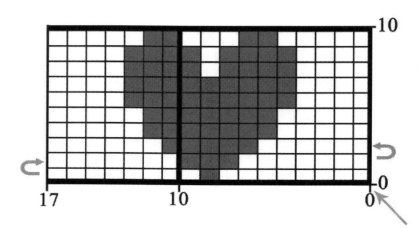

10

17 10 0

Start here
and work
across

Changing colours;

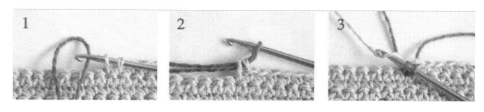

Do not finish the last dc before changing colours, leave two loops on your hook. Make a loose loop with your contrasting coloured yarn .

46

Pull the contrasting colour loop through the 2 loops on your hook. Carry on with the next stitch with the contrasting colour leaving all tails behind the work.

To change back to the previous colour, follow steps 1 and 2 picking up the main colour yarn.

When you have finished your heart motif, you can cut your contrasting coloured yarn, but leave enough of a tail to weave in later.

It is very important to keep a good tension on the yarn that will cross with back of your heart motif, do not pull it tightly, as it will pucker your work and it wont lie flat. However don't leave it too loose as this will make your stitches become loose over time.

Back   *Front*

Row 42-45;

1ch, work 1dc in each stitch across to end, turn.

Row 46;

3ch (represents 1tr, 1ch), miss 1st dc, * 1tr in next dc, 1ch, miss 1 dc * rpt frm * til end working last tr in turning ch (9 1ch spaces). Turn.

Row 47;

1ch, 1dc in 1st 1 ch space, 1dc in each tr and 1 ch space til end working last dc in top of turning ch. Turn (17dc in total).

Row 48-51;

1ch, 1dc in each dc across til end. Fasten off and weave in all ends.

Fold your gift bag in half, wrong sides together, and use a simple running stitch down each side with the main colour yarn making sure that the tr rows line up.

Finally using the ribbon of your choice, weave it in and out of your tr row, round the back and then the front.

Ta-dah! You have your very own heart gift bag perfect for giving that special gift for Valentines Day (or Birthday or Christmas or any occasion actually!) :)

Made in the USA
Middletown, DE
07 June 2024

55437606R00033